IMAGES
of America

MOUNT ST. HELENS

This c. 1908 photograph shows a group of young people heading out to explore Ole's Cave in the lava beds on the south side of Mount St. Helens. The cave, a lava tube, was an early tourist attraction, as was its discoverer, Ole Peterson. (Courtesy of Walter Hanson; photograph by Wilfred Craik.)

ON THE COVER: Mount St. Helens, often compared with Fujiyama in Japan because of its symmetrical cone shape, looms above a couple enjoying the day fishing at Spirit Lake in the 1960s. The Spirit Lake that existed before 1980—along with its cabins, campgrounds, and lodges—is now under 210 feet of landslide material and water. (Courtesy of the US Forest Service.)

IMAGES
of America

MOUNT ST. HELENS

David A. Anderson

ARCADIA
PUBLISHING

Published by Arcadia Publishing
Charleston, South Carolina

Printed in the United States of America

Library of Congress Control Number: 2013934945

For all general information, please contact Arcadia Publishing:
Telephone 843-853-2070
Fax 843-853-0044
E-mail sales@arcadiapublishing.com
For customer service and orders:
Toll-Free 1-888-313-2665

Visit us on the Internet at www.arcadiapublishing.com

To the staff and volunteers of the Mount St. Helens National Volcanic Monument and Mount St. Helens Institute who help maintain, interpret, and keep a really unique place accessible to everyone.

CONTENTS

ACKNOWLEDGMENTS

As with any large undertaking, there are many people who have enabled this project to evolve from a collection of old postcards into an assemblage of photographs that try to illustrate what Mount St. Helens was like prior to May 18, 1980. Rick McClure, Heritage and Tribal Programs manager for the Gifford Pinchot National Forest, generously provided access to the photographic archives of Gifford Pinchot National Forest. Photographs from the US Forest Service's archives are identified herein with "USFS." Matthew Sloan, who is a passionate collector of photographic images of the mountain, opened up his vast collection of postcards, slides, and photographs; his photographs are identified as "Sloan." Walter Hanson provided the opportunity to copy the real-photo postcards made by Wilfred Craik. Craik's photographs from the early 1900s are truly amazing. It is too bad Craik was unable to make a living at photography. Without the contributions of these three people, this book would not have been possible.

I would also like to thank Megan Moholtz, who generously provided photographs from the Weyerhaeuser Company archives; Steve Kinney, who opened up his collection of postcards; and Mark Moore, Susan Saul, Peter Frenzen, Carolyn Driedger, Richard Waitt, Roberta and Frank Emerick, and Ernie Schaffran, who all answered questions and provided background information. Photographs or postcards from the author's collection are identified as "Anderson."

INTRODUCTION

The eruption of Mount St. Helens on May 18, 1980, suddenly and drastically changed a mountain and the landscape around it. At the same time, it also changed how we look at the volcanoes of the Cascade Range. Eruptions of volcanoes were no longer something that happened somewhere else, or at some nearly forgotten time in the past. Eruptions were now something that could happen in our backyards and in our lifetimes.

Sadly and unfortunately, 57 people lost their lives that day. Several people were severely injured but survived. Some people who lost a loved one or a favorite summer cabin cannot bring themselves to go back—the pain is just too great. For others, those events in 1980 and since provide an amazing opportunity to study and learn about the geological and biological processes that have helped shape the Cascade Range and the environment that nearby inhabitants live in today.

We may have forgotten what our backyard volcanoes are capable of doing, but the scientists who were studying them before 1980 realized that Mount St. Helens was the most active of the Cascade peaks and was also the most likely to erupt before the end of the 20th century—and it did.

I grew up in Humboldt County, California, where people are frequently awakened at night by the trembling of an earthquake. It was therefore easy to become fascinated by the movements of the earth's crust. In the late 1960s, a map showing earthquake epicenters of the region highlighted a concentration along the Mendocino Escarpment, which runs nearly east/west off Cape Mendocino. A straight line drawn eastward from the escarpment would nearly hit Mount Lassen, the only other volcano in the 48 contiguous states that has erupted in the 20th century. Why are there major volcanoes north of that line, but none south of it? Plate tectonics and continental drift answer that question.

The earth's surface is composed of huge plates that slowly move around. In some places, the plates slide past each other like they do along California's San Andreas Fault. Sometimes the plates bump in to each other, like India is doing to Asia, and a huge mountain range like the Himalayas is the result. And sometimes, one plate dives beneath another, like what is happening along the North American coastline north of Cape Mendocino. As one plate moves beneath another, the subducting plate begins to melt, and that melt becomes magma and rises towards the earth's surface. Sometimes the magma reaches the surface and erupts and then is called lava. Sometimes eruptions are explosive—like the one that happened at Mount St. Helens in 1980.

Volcanic activity and glaciers molded and carved the spectacular landscape that surrounded Mount St. Helens before 1980. But geological processes were slow and took time to develop—or so we thought. After all, glaciers—like the ones that covered the highlands 140,000 years ago and extended in the Lewis River Valley to within five miles of the present-day location of Interstate 5 at Woodland—melted long ago.

The native peoples who colonized the land at least 7,000 years ago learned over time how to utilize the abundant resources from the forests, meadows, lakes, and streams that existed when they arrived. Everything had a spirit, and the mountains were personified. A specific mountain might be a man with two wives or a woman with two suitors. The stories told and retold of creation, morals, and people's places in the universe. The immediate area around Mount St. Helens and Spirit Lake was avoided for the most part, and why would a group not want to avoid a place that was totally unpredictable? The geological record indicates fairly frequent volcanic activity during the last 4,000 years, which ranged from large explosive eruptions to fluid lava flows at Mount St. Helens, or, as the natives called it, Lawetlat'la—the smoker.

After the arrival of Europeans, there were volcanic eruptions in the area, which were accurately portrayed by several artists and noted in journals. But the remote mountain was difficult to reach due to the rough terrain and thick temperate rain forests. There were some trails used by native peoples over the millennia, but it would still take three days of hard travel to reach Spirit Lake from Castle Rock.

People like Robert Lange headed inland in search of a living. His goal, and the goal of others like him, was to create a means to haul out the natural resources within the fertile area. Roads followed trails, while flumes and railroads were built to move resources and people at increasing speeds and distances. The impact of man on the land dramatically intensified with the arrival of the Europeans.

People like Ole Peterson headed inland to escape to the solitude of the mountains and the policies of Pres. Grover Cleveland. Peterson found a lava tube on his land that became a tourist attraction—Ole's Cave. Peterson was a fixture in the Lewis River Valley, much as Harry Truman, or Truman as he was known, was to Spirit Lake. Peterson later died from burns he suffered after he entered his house during a fire to try to recover some belongings. Truman died at his lodge during the initial stages of the 1980 eruption of Mount St. Helens.

Spirit Lake, the deep, cold, blue lake at the foot of Mount St. Helens, was about as picturesque a spot as could be found anywhere. The YMCA, Boy Scouts, Girl Scouts, and Episcopal Church had summer camps at the lake. The campers spent a lot of time outdoors, and daily hikes conditioned youngsters for attempts at summiting the mountain. The area around the lake contained at least 50 summer homes and several campgrounds that enabled people to spend time away from the modern world. People paid good money for a boat ride to Harmony Falls Lodge and several nights' stay in a rustic cabin that had oil lamps (no electricity), a bucket for a privy, homemade food, and a view that beat all. Life was good.

Then all that changed in the blink of an eye in 1980, with the 48 contiguous states' largest volcanic eruption of the 20th century. In a matter of seconds on the morning of May 18, the largest landslide in recorded history fell off the north side of the mountain. Portions of it flew across the Spirit Lake basin, where deposits can be seen at the north end of the west arm; another portion overtopped Johnston Ridge and flowed down Coldwater Creek, while the majority, as deep as 600 feet, flowed down the North Fork of the Toutle River for approximately 15 miles. The landslide uncorked an unexpected horizontal blast that knocked over, pulverized, burned, or vaporized 230 square miles of mostly forested land.

This book does not concentrate on "the big one," but rather on what came before. It is mostly a compilation of photographs taken from all sides of the mountain that show what it was like before 1980, and what it will look like again one day.

One

THE SETTING

Perpetual Snow near Chehalis, Wash.

Geologically, Mount St. Helens is a young and very active stratovolcano. Although there has been volcanic activity in the area for millions of years, the mountain did not start to form until about 35,000 years ago, when domes erupted in the area. The Mount St. Helens that existed before the 1980 eruption—shown here on a 1909 postcard—was formed within the last 2,000 years. (Steve Kinney.)

On his voyage of exploration of the Pacific Ocean, Capt. George Vancouver saw and named the mountain after the Baron St. Helens, Alleyne Fitzherbert, who was then the British ambassador to Spain. Most know the mountain by that name today. Local native people also had names for the mountain. (Anderson.)

The Cowlitz people called the mountain Lawetlat'la, or "smoker," and regarded it and the lake at its base as very special places. Because of the frequent volcanic activity, native people generally did not venture onto the slopes of the mountain. The lake was also supposedly the realm of supernatural creatures, including a fish with a head like a bear. This illustration is from the February 17, 1866, edition of the *Illustrated London News*. (Anderson.)

Beautiful Washington. Mount St. Helens, 50 miles distant.

People have been using the land in the vicinity of Mount St. Helens for well over 5,000 years. Tribes in the region traveled on interconnected trails and would gather in the fall along the summit of the Cascades east of the mountain to gather huckleberries and to trade with each other. The land provided an abundance of resources upon which people could live. (Anderson.)

Mt. St. Helens from Mt. Rainier, Washington.

In the early 1800s, the first Caucasian explorers and trappers traveled along the trails made by native peoples. Those later explorers found a rugged land, which Gen. George McClellan thought to be "utterly worthless for any purpose." (Anderson.)

11

Beautiful Washington – Mount Baker
from Baker Lake. Alt. 10827 ft.

The Cascade Range stretches from southern British Columbia in the north all the way south to Mount Lassen in northern California. The northernmost major peak in Washington is Mount Baker, which was also named by Capt. George Vancouver after his third lieutenant, Joseph Baker. Koma Kulshan is a local tribal name for this mountain. (Anderson.)

No. 1219   Steaming Crater of Mt. Baker.
COPYRIGHT BY S. & C. 1903

Steam is frequently seen at Mount Baker's summit, but there has not been an eruption there since around 1843. There was an increase in gas and steam emissions in March 1975 that led to some melting of summit ice. The increase in emissions led to some concern that the mountain might erupt again, but it did not and has since remained quiet. (Anderson.)

Mount Lassen, in northern California, is the only other Cascade Range volcano to erupt in the 20th century. It was particularly active from 1914 to 1917. The largest explosion, in May 1915, sent an ash column up to 40,000 feet above the mountain. It is one of the largest dome-type volcanoes in the world. (Anderson.)

Mount Shasta, also in northern California, is the most voluminous of the Cascade volcanoes. After looking at the hummocks formed from the 1980 landslide at Mount St. Helens, scientists were able to interpret that the hills on the northwest side of Mount Shasta were also formed by the collapse of an ancestral Mount Shasta over 300,000 years ago. (Anderson.)

The caldera holding Crater Lake was formed by the collapse of a mountain we now call Mount Mazama. This eruption—much larger than the 1980 Mount St. Helens eruption—took place about 6,800 years ago and was probably witnessed by native people living in the area. It would have had a major negative impact on people and animals living downwind because of the large amount of ash and pumice deposited by the explosion. (Anderson.)

Lava tubes, like this one thought to be near Bend, Oregon, are located throughout the Cascades where basalt, a fluid type of lava, is found. The lava makes great insulation, and ice that persisted in some lava tubes into summer months allowed early setters to refrigerate food and beverages. There are several known lava tubes on the south side of Mount St. Helens. (Anderson.)

Climbers going into camp at Mt. Tacoma, near Tacoma, Wash.

5539. *I enjoy nursing very much. Dont know how to be cross any more. Please greet your people especially mother. H. M. S.*

Mount Rainier (formerly called Mount Tacoma) is considered by volcanologists to be one of the most dangerous mountains in the Cascade Range. Lahars originating at the mountain have traveled as far as Puget Sound, inundating areas along river bottoms that are now highly developed urban centers. (Anderson.)

ON THE ROAD FROM MOUNT RAINIER NATIONAL PARK, WASHINGTON

A trip to the Cascades in the very early 20th century was an expedition and might have involved multiple forms of transportation, including boat, train, horse-drawn buggies or wagons, and—if late enough—the automobile. A portion of the trip might also be by horseback or hiking beyond the end of an established road. (Anderson.)

15

Mount Hood, Oregon, is one of three large volcanic peaks that are the "Guardians of the Columbia." Mounts St. Helens and Adams in Washington are the other two. These three peaks play prominent roles in local native legends. These mountains were also recognized as special places because smoke, fire, and rocks issued from them at times. (Anderson.)

The rapids at Cascade Locks on the Columbia River play an important part in one myth that tells about a "Bridge of the Gods" that spanned the river at this point. The "bridge" was created when a landslide from Greenleaf Peak and Table Mountain temporarily dammed the Columbia. Benjamin A. Gifford of The Dalles published this postcard in 1908. (Anderson.)

The high Cascade peaks are ecological islands of alpine habitat surrounded by lower-elevation forest habitats. Fog forms when cool, moist marine air floods inland valleys, and the mountains stand out like islands above a sea of clouds. (Anderson; photograph by Charles S. Reeves.)

Mount Adams, located east of Mount St. Helens, is the largest—but not the tallest—of the Washington volcanoes. Although oral traditions of the native people tell of frequent fighting among the nearby volcanoes, there is no physical evidence indicating an eruption of Mount Adams since about 3,500 years ago. (Anderson.)

Mount St. Helens forms a prominent landmark about 45 miles north-northeast of Portland. It is one of five major Cascade peaks that can be seen from the city. The others are Mounts Rainier, Adams, Hood, and Jefferson. The proximity to Portland allows for viewers to witness explosive eruptions on clear days. Goat Mountain, one of the domes that was a precursor to the current mountain, is visible on the horizon at left. (Anderson.)

1202 Washington — Mt. St. Helens, 9750 feet.

18

Two

GETTING THERE

Mt. St Helens from St. Helens Ore.

Traveling from Portland to Mount St. Helens in the mid to late 1800s required a boat trip down the Columbia River to Kelso, a short rail journey to Castle Rock, and then an arduous overland trip up the Toutle River. It was a three-day journey by foot from Castle Rock to Spirit Lake. (Sloan.)

This is an unusual photograph of Mount St. Helens. The view of the mountain is from the southwest side in the area of Butte Camp. However, there never have been farms and buildings on this side of the mountain. It is unknown where the farms in the lower portion of the photograph are located. The photographer is unknown, but the photograph is probably from around 1910. (Sloan.)

Silver Lake was created about 2,500 years ago, when natural dams at Spirit Lake broke several times and sent massive lahars down the Toutle River Valley. These lahars blocked what is now called Outlet Creek, forming Silver Lake. During the late 19th century, people of European descent colonized the area around Silver Lake, clearing the forests and tilling the soils, as on this homestead on Carnine Road on the west side of Silver Lake. (Anderson.)

Fishing along the Toutle River is a very popular pastime. Anadromous fish are no longer able to use the North Fork Toutle River basin above the large sediment retention structure that was constructed after the 1980 eruption to stop mudflow debris from having an ongoing serious impact on the Cowlitz and Columbia Rivers below the Toutle. Siltation from the lahars from the 1980 eruption did reach the Columbia River, which was closed to shipping until the river was dredged. (Weyerhaeuser Archives.)

In 1948, Weyerhaeuser Company developed five company parks along the Toutle River, including the Coal Banks Park 13 miles east of Castle Rock. Here, members of the Oscar Weed and George Barker families, from Longview, cook hotdogs over the campfire. The upper park was at Marratta Creek, five miles below Spirit Lake. In 1954, the Coal Banks site was renamed and rededicated for Harry Morgan, manager for the Company's Longview Lumber Division, who was instrumental in setting up these parks. The seven-acre park was rebuilt in 1974 to meet newer standards and opened as a day-use facility. The park, like other company facilities along the Toutle River, was heavily damaged or destroyed by the lahars in 1980. (Weyerhaeuser Archives.)

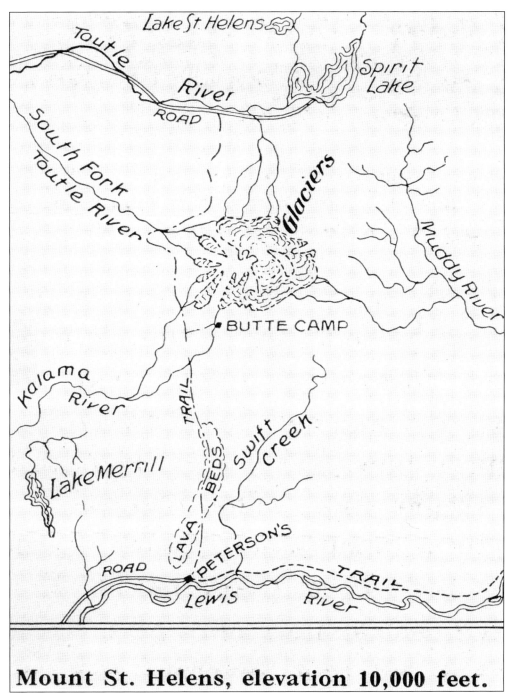

Mount St. Helens, elevation 10,000 feet.

In 1912, few roads could be found around the mountain. Along the North Fork Toutle River, a road went as far as Spirit Lake, while in the Lewis River Valley, on the south side, a road went only as far as Ole Peterson's ranch east of what is now Cougar. Trails originally made by native peoples connected the two roads and went on up the Lewis River Valley. This map is from *The Guardians of the Columbia*, which was published in 1912. (Anderson).

Hoffstedt Creek on the County Road from St. Helens Post Office in Cowlitz Co. to Spirit Lake in Skamania Co., Wash.

The first wagon road up the Toutle River Valley towards Spirit Lake was constructed in 1901. From Castle Rock, it was "completed for a distance of about 27 or 28 miles," as reported in the *Morning Oregonian* in August 1901. At the end of the road there were another 10 to 12 miles of trail and a boat ride across Spirit Lake to reach the mines on the north shore. Prior to the construction of the first wagon road, it would take prospectors and explorers three days to hike from Castle Rock to Spirit Lake. (Anderson.)

The current Spirit Lake Highway (State Highway 504) was built after the 1980 eruption's landslide and lahars buried the road that followed the bottom of the canyon. It now takes people about an hour to travel the same distance that once required three days of hiking. The lower end of the bridge, pictured in 2009, is at the western edge of the 1980 blast zone, some 14 miles from the crater. (Anderson.)

On The Way Up
Lewis River Valley No.70

Roads traveling up the Lewis River on the south side of the mountain reached several miles east of Cougar and ended at Ole Peterson's ranch near the present-day Swift Reservoir Dam. This photograph was taken in the early 20th century. (Walter Hanson collection; photograph by Wilfred Craik.)

In this 1909 photograph, a car makes its way across rubbly pumice on the road to Spirit Lake near the Robert Lange homestead. Cars cut traveling time from Castle Rock to Spirit Lake from three days—when hiking in—down to just under six hours. That, at the time, was incredibly fast. (USFS.)

In the 1930s, the road to Spirit Lake was still an unpaved one-lane road with a few wide spots. By 1941—when the headline to a story in *The Oregonian* proclaimed: "Once It Was a Trek That Would Fag A Mountain Goat, But Now It's Only Three Hours From Portland's Door"—road conditions had improved. The scenery of the Mount St. Helens region was touted as being wilder, more picturesque, and more commanding than the scenery around Mount Hood, Oregon. (USFS.)

Cataboo Cabin, with Georgia Lange sitting outside, was a store built by the Langes at the outlet to Spirit Lake. Logs floating on the lake are visible in the background. This spot also had the landing, which serviced the mines on the lake's north shore. Harry Truman later had his Mount St. Helens Lodge on this site. (USFS.)

Homesteading on the upper Toutle canyon was difficult at best. While the Langes made a go of it, others could not. The soil was poor and full of boulders. In this image, Forest Guard Sethe is inspecting Louis Bright's homestead claim, which was deserted by October 1909. (USFS.)

The Spirit Lake Lodge was built around 1941 by Harry and Julia (Lange) Gustafson on the Lange Homestead about a mile west of Spirit Lake. They advertised souvenirs, home-cooked meals, country-style fried chicken, and homemade pies. The Langes were also noted for their huckleberry pies. In May 1956, the lodge was available to lease for only $2,500 down, along with 60 acres, a picnic ground, 10 rooms, cabins, a gas station, a restaurant, and more. (Both, Sloan.)

At times local lodge managers, their family, and neighbors would gather in the basement's furnace room and enjoy drinking whiskey and trading stories. Bottles would be brought and, if not finished off, left for another time. One local permanent resident was Jim Lund, whose smile always sparkled because of an emerald in a front tooth. Jim, who always had a joke to tell, was also deaf, but could read lips. As the night wore on and the bottles got emptier, Jim would ask people to talk slower so he could follow the conversation, recalls Ernie Schaffran. (Steve Kinney.)

A dam installed at the outlet of Spirit Lake around 1900 raised the lake's water level about three feet and was named after Dr. Henry W. Coe, who had it built to regulate the lake. Dr. Coe was also active with the mines on the north shore and, later, with recreation at the lake. (USFS.)

402370

For the most part, there were no views of the mountain on the trip up the Toutle River, since the tall forest generally blocked the view. Even after reaching Spirit Lake's south shore, the mountain remained out of sight. It was not until one was out in a boat on the lake that the mountain became visible. This view is from the head of the Toutle River. (USFS.)

Spirit Lake first formed about 3,350 years ago, when pyroclastic flows from the growing Mount St. Helens dammed the Toutle River. When water in the lake reached a critical point, the debris dam would break, resulting in a lahar that would flow down the Toutle River to the Columbia River via the Cowlitz River. The process of filling and draining has been repeated several times. (Sloan.)

The first white homesteaders were there to make a living off the forests and minerals found in and around the lake. Mining was difficult, since the ore had to be barged across the lake and then hauled down rough wagon roads to the nearest railroad. Efforts were made to push a rail line up to Spirit Lake to support mining, but the rails never quite reached the lake. (Sloan.)

Mount St. Helens is a stratovolcano, which is a volcano composed of loose rock and ash interbedded with lava flows and domes. Prior to 1980, the mountain was about 9,677 feet in elevation. It lost about 1,300 feet on May 18, 1980, and since then has lost at least another 100 feet in elevation due to sloughing of the crater walls. (Anderson.)

Beautiful Washington – Mount St. Helens, Alt. 9,750 ft.   *Mar. 3. 09*

The local native people believed that Spirit Lake was inhabited by spirits of the dead, which could be seen in the form of fog rising from the lake or in a chance reflection in the calm, still waters. The fish that did inhabit the lake were not eaten, because it was believed that they had the spirit of the dead in them, and that some fish had bear heads and cougar fangs. The mountain remains an important cultural and religious icon to neighboring tribes. (USFS.)

In an October 1878 letter to the *Morning Oregonian*, L.J. Davis described a five-week trip that he took in the country of the Cowlitz, Klickitat, and Toutle Rivers with Judge T.M. Pearson of Lewis County, Washington. Even though they were unable to reach the summit of Mount St. Helens because of the compacted ice, they wrote that the view from the mountain was "but a mere confusion of ragged peaks" and the scenery "grand in the extreme." Davis predicted that Mount St. Helens "is bound to be at no distant day one of the leading summer resorts on the Pacific coast." (Sloan.)

Probably the most notorious lodge operator at Spirit Lake was the curmudgeon named Harry Truman. Truman, as he was called, operated the Mount St. Helens Lodge on the south shore of Spirit Lake starting around 1926. He liked his whiskey (even during Prohibition), and cats, but he was not particularly fond of children. Ernie Schaffran recalled that he made a point to shovel snow around Truman's lodge. He was offered a soda in payment but refused it, and was told "Don't come back, yur stirrin' up ma cats." It became an annual event to do a good deed, since he knew it bugged Truman. When Truman and his wife arrived at Spirit Lake in 1926, he went into business with Jack Nelson, who ran a store and gas station on the south shore. The two men had personalities that clashed. They fought over how each treated the customers and over the rental boats. In 1928, Nelson sold out to Truman and started a lodge at Harmony Falls on the northeast side of the lake. (Both, Sloan.)

Tourists could rent Harry Truman's cabins along the southern shoreline, while the seasonal summer help slept in the boathouse. People either got along with Truman, or they did not; it seems there was no happy medium. During the Columbus Day storm in 1962, a lot of damage was incurred around the Spirit Lake basin. Trees were blown down and removed around the Mount St. Helens Lodge, which opened up the view of the mountain from the shoreline. (Both, Sloan.)

Recreational use of the Spirit Lake basin increased while mining decreased, and recreation eventually became the main focus for the north side of the mountain. Mount St. Helens, Spirit Lake, and the Mount Margaret Backcountry saw more recreational use than any other area in the Gifford Pinchot National Forest. By 1979, there were 480,000 visitor days in the area. (USFS.)

Two young fishermen take time to get their bearings by inspecting the recreation map at Spirit Lake. The map on the sign guided visitors to trails that led to the lakes in the Mount Margaret Backcountry, and helped hikers get to the Plains of Abraham and Ape Canyon. (USFS.)

Spirit Lake was a popular venue for campers. It allowed families an affordable means to spend some time in nature. The style of tents changed little from the 1930s to the 1960s; they were commonly made of canvas with a center pole for support. (USFS.)

The Spirit Lake Campground was very popular, and frequently full, during the short camping season at Spirit Lake. The campground, which had 173 units in 1969, could handle 620 people at one time. Three much smaller campgrounds on the east side of the lake could each handle up to 60 people at a time and were accessible only by foot or boat. (USFS.)

This photograph shows Spirit Lake Campground in the 1950s. There were no nearby public telephones, and in 1969, the closest (public pay) phone was reported to be 26 miles away. A Land Management Plan was issued in the fall of 1979 for Gifford Pinchot National Forest, but those plans were put on hold after the eruption in the spring of 1980. (Sloan.)

Washington State annually stocked rainbow trout at Spirit Lake, providing recreational opportunities for many. A few trout weighed up to seven pounds and measured 26 inches. Although salmon migrated up the Toutle River to the Spirit Lake basin, they were not to be taken from that area. (USFS.)

Young fishermen clean
their catch on a dock
while the peaks of
the Mount Margaret
Backcountry rise in the
background. (USFS.)

Forest Ranger
Robert J. Stekiel
takes time to inspect
a nice fish caught by
a camper at Spirit
Lake. Rainbow,
eastern brook, and
large cutthroat trout
were in the lake; the
cutthroats sometimes
weighed as much
as six pounds and
were two feet in
length. (USFS.)

SPIRIT LAKE
RECREATION AREA
1936

COLUMBIA
NATIONAL FOREST
U. S. DEPT. OF AGRICULTURE
FOREST SERVICE
REGION – 6
GUIDE NO. 6   WASH.

Although Mount St. Helens was initially left out, much of the area east of the mountain became a forest reserve in 1897 thanks to the US Department of the Interior. Mount St. Helens was added later, and the forest reserves were transferred to the US Department of Agriculture in 1905. The forest reserve became known as the Columbia National Forest in 1908. In 1959, the name was changed to the Gifford Pinchot National Forest in honor of the first chief of the US Forest Service. (USFS.)

The ranger station buildings improved over time from the early abandoned homesteader's cabin. Offices, residences and dorms, shops, garages, and a dock were built at the southern shore of Spirit Lake—all to support land management activities. (USFS.)

An early ranger's residence was a small cabin, which would have been luxurious when compared with the abandoned homesteader's cabin that was first used as a ranger's residence. (USFS.)

A mess hall was needed to feed the number of people employed by the US Forest Service during the summer season. The number of employees increased in the summer to help maintain the recreational facilities around the lake and mountain, as well as to help fight forest fires. (USFS.)

The placement of garbage cans at recreation sites did not necessarily mean the public would use them. However, a bear could be a problem, since it would tip over garbage cans and possibly raid unattended food left out by campers. (USFS.)

With bags and boxes full of trash in the background, Boy Scouts received recognition from the US Forest Service for having picked up garbage left behind by some forest users. Volunteers continue to play an important role in the operation and maintenance of the Mount St. Helens National Volcanic Monument. (USFS.)

The Youth Conservation Corps was a program created in 1970 that employed teenagers during the summer to help maintain facilities on federal public lands. Here, a group of young men works on a project at the Spirit Lake Campground. Due to budget cuts, the program was discontinued in 1982. (USFS.)

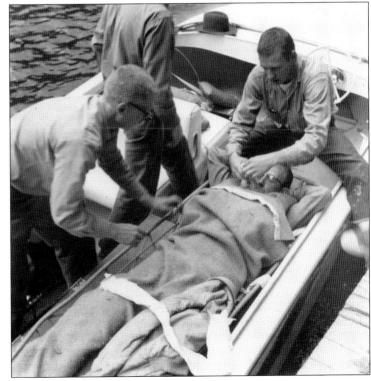

Although they are infrequent, accidental injuries and, unfortunately, deaths—especially for those who are not properly equipped to climb the mountain—happen, and it is necessary for US Forest Service employees to be trained and ready to help evacuate the injured. (USFS.)

An improved Duck Bay boat ramp (under construction in these images) allowed 250 people to use this recreational spot in one day. Mountains of the rugged Mount Margaret Backcountry rise in the background to elevations of over 5,800 feet. (Both, USFS.)

The Duck Bay boat launch facility is shown here on a busy summer's day. Once winter snow melted, sometimes as late as mid-June, the boat launch and neighboring campground would be busy with boaters and fishermen. (Both, USFS.)

This is how the US Forest Service transported their boat, the *St. Helens*, to the lake before boat trailers were invented. The boat was used to transport US Forest Service employees around the lake as part of their duties. (USFS.)

With the *St. Helens* in the water, a group of US Forest Service employees prepare to travel across the lake to inspect mines that had closed on the north shore. (USFS.)

Here, some well-dressed people wait at the dock in Spirit Lake in the 1930s. In 1949, the *Seattle Times* touted the area, saying that it "leaves nothing to be desired in the way of fun, and variety of things to do." Currently, scientific research into biological and geological processes is taking priority over recreation in the Spirit Lake basin, although the US Forest Service still allows some recreational uses. (USFS.)

This view towards the Duck Bay dock from offshore illustrates how it was not possible to see the mountain from the southern lakeshore because of the tall trees. (USFS.)

Because of the tall trees lining the south shore of Spirit Lake, the mountain was generally not visible until a boat was far offshore or a hiker had gone far enough north along the trail. This boat has sailed from the US Forest Service's dock. Some of the Spirit Lake ranger station's buildings are visible among the trees along the shore. (USFS, photograph by Leland J. Prater, 1949.)

Spirit Lake was open to many kinds of boats and boating, with options ranging from canoes to sailboats to powerboats with water skiers in tow; water sports were popular in the lake's cold waters. (USFS.)

This family is crossing Spirit Lake toward the Mount St. Helens Lodge complex, with Mount St. Helens towering above. (Washington Digital Archives, photograph AR-28001001-ph001745.)

Jack Nelsons—Harmony Falls, Wn.

Harmony Falls was the spot on the lake where Jack Nelson built his lodge after he sold his share of the Mount St. Helens Lodge to Harry Truman in 1928. He and his wife, Tressa, built their lodge on the northeast shore of the lake. There were no roads to the lodge, only a trail through the forest or a boat ride across the lake. The falls are no longer visible, since they are now beneath Spirit Lake's waters. (Steve Kinney.)

Guests stayed in individual cabins, while the Nelsons and their help used rooms in the lodge. To keep food chilled, it was kept in pots held in the water below the falls. The Harmony Falls lodge was known and loved for its rustic atmosphere and attracted a faithful following of Portland families each year. (USFS.)

In 1908, the YMCA started holding an annual pilgrimage to Spirit Lake. Initially, the YMCA launch took campers to Castle Rock and arrived about noon the day they left Portland. It would then take another two and a half days of walking, while their gear traveled by wagon, to reach the lake. In 1921, it cost $17.50 for boys to attend the YMCA summer camp, and that included 115 miles of transportation each way. In 1932, the YMCA renamed its camp at Spirit Lake Camp Meehan after the founder of the camp, J.C. Meehan. The lodge at the original YMCA camp was on the south shore. The Episcopal Diocese of Olympia bought the YMCA camp and moved it to the northeast side of the lake after purchasing land from Dr. Henry Coe. (Both, USFS.)

The Boy Scout camp was located at the north shore of the east arm of the lake, while the Girl Scouts had their camp just a short distance away. Outdoor skills, camping, hiking, swimming, and target practice were all highlights of the Boy Scout summer camp experience at Spirit Lake. (USFS; photographs by Pete Trotgott.)

Part of the fun of any summer camp, in addition to the camaraderie of being with other people your own age, was learning plant and animal identification. (USFS; photo by Pete Trotgott.)

Hiking is still a popular activity in the area, as it was prior to the 1980 eruption. Here, a group of children at the Spirit Lake ranger station are inspected prior to setting out on an overnight hike into the Mount Margaret Backcountry, which contains over 30 small lakes. (USFS.)

Mount St. Helens and Spirit Lake sold many products. The image of the mountain above the lake was used on the covers of road maps, dinner menus on trains, and liquor advertisements. Here, several young women pose for a photographer. (Washington Digital Archives, photograph AR-28001001-ph001744.)

Spirit Lake's water was not always blue, but sometimes looked green as it reflected the old fir trees that grew on the slopes surrounding the lake. (Washington Digital Archives, photograph AR-07809001-ph003890.)

The summer camp experience at Spirit Lake is now a thing of the past. The sound of Harmony Falls is silenced. In its place, however, is the chance to watch and learn about the infrequent sudden and dramatic natural transformation of landscapes caused by volcanic activity in the Cascade Range. Eruptive activity at Mount St. Helens 2,500 years ago and again around 1500 A.D. helped form and enlarge Spirit Lake. In the early 20th century, attempts were made by capitalists from Portland to develop a hydroelectric project at Spirit Lake and a small dam was constructed at the head of the Toutle River to help regulate stream flow. It was hoped that a dam 12 feet in height would provide electricity that could be sold to Portland, Tacoma, and Seattle. (Right, Washington Digital Archives, photograph AR-07809001-ph003893; below, USFS, photograph by Leland J. Prater, 1949.)

Several submerged trees were visible in the lake. These trees were killed in the eruption around 1500 A.D. that enlarged the lake. One at the north end of the lake was standing in 96 feet of water. (Steve Kinney.)

MOUNT SAINT HELENS

Majestically rising above Spirit Lake in Southwest Washington, is one of the state's four major peaks in the Cascade Range. Others are Mount Rainier, Mount Adams and Mount Baker, all over 10,000 feet.

Images of Spirit Lake with Mount St. Helens in the background were widely used to advertise products and to lure tourists to the state. Cards handed out at no charge by the Washington State Advertising and Progress Commissions used images of Mount St. Helens and Spirit Lake to attract visitors and future residents to the state. (Anderson.)

Three

TIMBERLINE AND CLIMBING

A wagon road up to Timberline on the north side of Mount St. Helens existed as early as around 1914, when Robert Lange worked on extending the road beyond Spirit Lake to Timberline. In 1945, the road to Spirit Lake was mostly paved, and a relaxing round-trip sightseeing trip from Portland, according to the *Sunday Oregonian*, could be done in just nine hours. The final leg from Spirit Lake to Timberline was not paved until 1962. This photograph was taken in April 1977. (Anderson; photograph by George Anderson.)

In August 1943, the Timberline parking area was a lightly defined area. In June 1941, *The Oregonian* described the last leg to Timberline as "narrow and winding, yet it is safe and can be negotiated in second-gear. Trees guard the precipitous drops. No traveler will get dizzy." (USFS.)

Cars in the yet-unpaved Timberline parking lot, including what appears to be a 1958 Edsel, overlook the west arm of Spirit Lake and the Mount Margaret Backcountry. (USFS.)

The aerial view from 1965 shows the large parking area and turnaround at Timberline, both of which were built in 1962 to handle the increasing number of climbers, hikers, and tourists. The parking area was used in 1980 by scientists taking measurements after the mountain began to reawaken. (USFS.)

In this c. 1960 image, a boy is all smiles after spending a day hiking on the mountain. (Washington Digital Archives, photograph AR-07809001-ph003892.)

Members of this group of hikers are carrying snowshoes on a spring outing around 1960. It was possible to go skiing above Timberline in the mornings and then finish the day fishing on Spirit Lake. (Sloan.)

On a late fall day, a hiker gazes upward at Dogs Head, Forsyth Glacier, and the False Summit of Mount St. Helens. (USFS.)

This 1930s image shows a view from Timberline up to Dogs Head and the Forsyth Glacier. The Forsyth Glacier is named after C.E. Forsyth of Castle Rock, who led a Mazamas Mountaineering Club rescue party in 1908 from the north side of the mountain to the south side, where John Anderson, a climber, had been seriously injured. The easiest way to bring Anderson out was to carry him up and over the mountain from the south side and back down to Spirit Lake on the north side. (USFS.)

This view from the Timberline parking lot looks up at Dogs Head (at left) and Forsyth Glacier in the late fall or early winter. (Sloan.)

This photograph looks down from above Timberline at the Timberline parking lot. Windy Ridge is immediately behind the lot, while the Smith Creek drainage is beyond. Except for the farthest ridges, nearly all of the landscape in this photograph was inside the 1980 blast zone, and the trees were pulverized, blown over, or burned to death. (USFS.)

The False Summit is the highest point in this photograph, but not on the mountain. After reaching the False Summit, climbers on the north route would have to cross a fairly flat ice field in the summit crater before reaching the true summit of Mount St. Helens. (USFS.)

This is the view from the Loowit Trail towards Windy Pass and Windy Ridge. Windy Ridge is aptly named, since the wind seems to be always blowing across the ridge. In 1980, despite its proximity to the mountain, this spot received more damage from the initial blast and subsequent pyroclastic flows than it did from the landslide. (USFS.)

The Spirit Lake ranger station was where climbers would register before and after making the climb to the summit of the mountain. Signs at the trailhead also advised climbers to only attempt the ascent if they were well trained and equipped with "proper clothing, food, and gear" should they need to spend the night if bad weather developed. (USFS.)

Outdoor activity is fraught with danger, whether it is working in a mine and losing an arm in a rockfall, as happened to George Williams, or performing a heroic rescue and getting a glacier named after you, as happened to C.E. Forsyth. The Forest Service posted signs like this at the head of climbing routes on the mountain, warning would-be climbers to be properly prepared. (USFS.)

In 1908, Wilfred Craik captured this image of a group of climbers who probably ascended from the southwest side of the mountain via Butte Camp. Although the group is not roped together, wearing crampons, or carrying packs with supplies, they are wearing long-sleeved shirts and hats to protect from sunburn. (Walter Hanson; photograph by Wilfred Craik.)

These climbers ascending the Dogs Head route are roped together. The view is northerly, with Spirit Lake in the center, Windy Ridge to its right, and Mount Rainier on the horizon. In 1968, US Forest Service maps advised visitors that the road at the top of the clear cut in the background would be closed to public traffic during periods of heavy log hauling. (USFS.)

Snow Crevice
Mt St. Helens Wh.

In a story in the *Morning Oregonian* of April 8, 1888, about a climb to the summit of Mount St. Helens that year, W.B. Gilbert described the summit snow field as being almost level. He theorized that the snow field probably filled the entire crater, but he had no way of knowing how deep that was. He found the crevasses present in the summer to be from 20 to 30 feet deep. Gilbert said the snow "will remain undisturbed and unmoved until some day the volcanic fires that slumber below shall again warm this great cup and its chalice shall pour forth fire and ashes as of old." Little did he know that his prophecy would come true. (Both, Walter Hanson, photographs by Wilfred Craik.)

What are most likely annual snow layers appear very clearly in this 1908 photograph taken by Wilfred Craik. The dark layers are probably the windblown ash from late summer, when exposed bare ground is at its maximum. (Walter Hanson; photograph by Wilfred Craik.)

Members of the 1908 party take time out to explore the depth of a crevasse on the mountain's summit. (Walter Hanson; photograph by Wilfred Craik.)

In 1916, A.E. Cohoon, supervisor of the Columbia National Forest, proposed the construction of a fire lookout at the summit of Mount St. Helens. Construction started in 1918 and was not completed until 1921. The fire lookout was a 12-foot-square wooden building with a six-foot-square cupola on top. The idea of using steel cable and rock counterweights to haul the building materials up the side of the mountain apparently did not work as planned, since materials were carried up on the backs of the men hired to construct the lookout. (USFS.)

The men involved in the construction of the fire lookout lived in a camp established on top of the Goat Rocks. Although it was precariously situated, this spot allowed fairly easy access to the summit and the lookout. (USFS.)

The lookout reported fires to the district office by telephone. They even reported a large fire in Portland in 1924. However, even in summer the weather at the summit is quite variable. Even in July, storms can coat the windows with ice, making it all but impossible to see out. Along with haze and low clouds, it was deemed impractical to continue operation of the summit lookout and it was abandoned around 1929 in favor of lower elevation stations. The glass windows and cupola were gone by 1975 when Rick McClure, Gifford Pinchot Forest archaeologist and Heritage Program manager, climbed the mountain. (Above, USFS; below, Kinney.)

The climb up Mount St. Helens is not technically challenging, but it did—and still does—require minimal equipment and being in shape. Some of the slopes are steep. This c. 1960 view looks to the northeast toward the Goat Rocks Wilderness Area. (Sloan.)

This view looks northeast from near the summit, with Spirit Lake at the base of the mountain, the snow-dotted peaks of the Mount Margaret Backcountry to the left, and Mount Rainier rising above the clouds on the far horizon. The Mount St. Helens Lodge complex at the head of the Toutle River is near the lower left corner of the lake. (Sloan.)

An area of seracs that existed in the Wishbone glacier is visible in this c. 1960 photograph. Also visible at left is the Floating Island lava flow, which was the last lava flow that issued from the mountain prior to 1980. (Sloan.)

The popularity of climbing Mount St. Helens can be judged not only by the number of people on the trail but also by the tracks in the snow near the summit in this c. 1960 image. Today, the number of climbers allowed to summit Mount St. Helens is limited to 100 per day, and they can only travel on the southern route. (Sloan.)

These climbers are passing a rock outcrop called "The Chimney," which was located on the summit crater's rim. The summit crater ice field was a nearly flat glacier a quarter of a mile across. Climbers on the north route would reach the False Summit on the north rim of the crater. However, the true summit was on the south rim. Some climbers would hike around the summit following the crater's rim to avoid crevasses in the summit glacier. (Sloan.)

This c. 1960 view looks east across the summit crater ice field of Mount St. Helens toward Mount Adams. The summit ice field emptied mostly to the southeast, feeding what was Shoestring Glacier, which was on the Gibraltar climbing route. This was a spring-only climbing route because of hazardous rock falls. (Sloan.)

The first documented ascent of Mount St. Helens was in 1853, when Thomas Dryer led a party to the summit. The Craik party made the climb in 1908 wearing little more than overalls, long-sleeved shirts, and straw bonnets and felt hats for protection from the sun. Walking sticks and a rifle were used for balance during the climb. It is unknown if this group carried the coffee pot up or if it was already at the summit. The tobacco tins probably contained the summit register for climbers to sign. (Walter Hanson; photograph by Wilfred Craik.)

Glissading down the snow fields speeds up the descent but also has dangers. Controlling the speed, whether by using the walking sticks or rifle butt, is vital to a safe descent. Members of the Craik party enjoyed themselves on their way down the mountain in 1908. (Walter Hanson; photograph by Wilfred Craik.)

Climbers descending the mountain are roped together for safety. They also need crampons, especially on steeper icy slopes, to help prevent slips and falls. (USFS.)

It was reported on August 28, 1909, in the *Bellingham Herald* that the youngest person yet to reach the summit of Mount St. Helens was five-year-old Hilda Hubbard of Kelso, Washington. Her older sister Helen, six, and Mildred Leischarst, eight, also reached the summit. The parents of the Hubbard girls, Mr. and Mrs. B.L. Hubbard and Mrs. A. Leischarst, were also in the climbing party. (Sloan.)

Four

MOUNT MARGARET BACKCOUNTRY

Fires are a part of the forest ecosystem. Native peoples used fires to promote the growth of huckleberries in some areas. One of the largest forest fires in the Spirit Lake basin was accidentally started when a smudge pot, used to discourage flies from biting horses at the Lange Mine, was knocked over in 1908. Dead trees from that fire can be seen in early photographs of the Mount Margaret area. (Anderson.)

These two views are from the Mount Margaret Backcountry, about nine miles north of the mountain. The postcard above, used in 1916, shows the pre-eruption profile, while the photograph below from 2009 shows the crater and growing Crater Glacier. The backcountry remains a popular hiking area, with spectacular views of Mounts Rainier and Adams as well as Crater Glacier. Crater Glacier is an anomaly in that it is a low elevation glacier that is actually growing. It is growing because it is in a north-facing crater that it is fed by avalanches from the crater walls. (Both, Anderson.)

US Forest Service employees are pictured here on an inspection trip into the backcountry in the 1930s. In the early days of the US Forest Service, before roads crisscrossed the forests, the forest ranger inspected the land on horseback. His duties included maintenance of phone lines and supervision of trail maintenance, construction, and the firefighting team. (USFS.)

This 1960s view from the Mount Margaret Backcountry shows the west arm of Spirit Lake, the Mount St. Helens Lodge complex, the north face of the mountain, and Butte Camp Dome (at right). (USFS.)

The Dome (5,707 feet), a prominent feature near Mount Margaret, was reachable by hiking about 4.5 miles of trail from Spirit Lake. It is still accessible by hiking or biking along the Boundary Trail. (USFS.)

The Mount Margaret Backcountry is an extremely rugged place that is accessible by trail. It is a highland underlain by intrusive granitic rocks. (USFS.)

Here, forest rangers check on the Mount Margaret Backcountry. There was not a trail that went around Spirit Lake at lake level. To make a loop hike around Spirit Lake required hiking 15 miles and climbing 2,200 feet in 4.5 miles up to Mount Margaret and past St. Helens Lake before dropping back down to Coe's Landing on the north shore. (USFS.)

St. Helens Lake is a large tarn in a cirque that was carved during a glacial advance from 22,000 to 11,000 years ago. It is the largest tarn in the Mount Margaret Backcountry and sits at an elevation of 4,567 feet. During this glaciation, valley glaciers reached a distance of 19 miles down the North Fork Toutle River Valley. (USFS.)

Before phone lines were installed in the forest, early fire guards might have to travel 23 miles to report a fire. The fire lookout on Coldwater Peak was constructed in 1936. In this photograph, horses from an inspection team are at the hitching post. (USFS.)

Prior to the 1980 eruption, there were about 15 mountain goats living in the backcountry. They were killed in the eruption, like all exposed living things. However, the population has bounced back, and mountain goats can once again be found in the backcountry and on Mount St. Helens. (USFS.)

In 1891, ore found at Spirit Lake prompted the creation of the St. Helens Mining District the following year. Work on mines on the north side of Spirit Lake attracted young men in search of jobs. George Williams (left), lost his right forearm in a mining accident at Robert Lange's mine and got a job in 1911 as the first full-time ranger at the Spirit Lake Ranger District. His monthly pay was $100, and he was required to furnish and feed three horses. His fire patrol district ranged from Meta Lake in the north, south through Spirit Lake and Goat Marsh to the Lewis River. He was required to perform trail maintenance, inspect homesteads and mining claims, and conduct boundary surveys. Erasmus Robertson (right) initially got a job building a flume at Spirit Lake, but he became a forest guard in 1909. (USFS.).

Dr. Henry W. Coe, who started the Morningside Hospital near Portland for the treatment of Alaska's mentally ill, was a great booster of the mining possibilities north of Spirit Lake and was involved with several mines. He attracted Teddy Roosevelt as an investor, while Robert Lange went to Germany to find backers for his mining operation. (USFS.)

Ore from the mines north of Spirit Lake had to be barged across the lake and then sent by wagon down the North Fork Toutle River. In 1901, Cowlitz County was spending a lot of money to build a road out of Castle Rock that would divert ore shipments from Chehalis to Castle Rock, where the ore would travel by rail to smelters in Portland. (USFS.)

"Sacajawea," the Pioneer Mother of Oregon, Monument erected in her memory by women of the United States, City Park, Portland, Oregon.

The Sacajawea statue that now stands in Washington Park in Portland was made from ore from Dr. Henry Coe's Sweden Mine. Sacajawea played an important role in helping to guide Lewis and Clark during their expedition to the Pacific coast. (Anderson.)

This is a view from the alpine meadows of the Mount Margaret Backcountry looking south over the west arm of Spirit Lake and the Mount St. Helens Lodge. It is easy to see how prehistoric avalanches, lahars, and pyroclastic flows came off the north side of the mountain and blocked what was later named the Toutle River, forming Spirit Lake. (USFS.)

In this c. 1982 photograph, the landscape appears bleak and barren with few plants growing in the loose, ashy soil. Two organisms that have helped shape the evolution of Mount St. Helens' post-1980 landscape are lupine, because it helps fix nitrogen in the soil, and the pocket gopher, which helps to spread seeds. (USFS.)

The blast zone initially looked like a barren landscape devoid of all life; however, this was not completely true. Deep winter snow that did not melt, especially on the lee side of the ridges, provided protection for both plants and small animals. These areas served as islands from which life spread to the surrounding barren landscape. The dark areas on the slopes above Norway Pass in the image above from 1985 are actually vegetation that survived the 1980 blast because they were protected by deep snow. Fireweed (at lower left above) was a common plant that colonized the blast zone soon after the eruption. The 2009 photograph below from the same location shows that the blown-down trees are rotting and returning their nutrients to the soil, enabling huckleberry, willows, conifers, and other plants to flourish. (Both, Anderson.)

Five

WINTER

Heavy winter snowfall on Mount St. Helens led to the formation of large glaciers, especially on the north side. These glaciers, along with the previous winter's snow pack, melted during the 1980 eruption and mixed with rock and ash to form the lahars that especially impacted the Toutle River valley. Smaller lahars were also found on other sides of the mountain as well. (Sloan.)

If the road to Timberline was not plowed, this parking area at Spirit Lake, pictured here in 1964, would be full of cars of winter visitors. (USFS.)

Goat Rocks, formed in the 19th century, are on the upper skyline. They were part of the 1980 landslide. This photograph was taken at the Timberline parking lot in 1964. (USFS.)

This photograph shows the plowing of the Timberline Road in 1964. (USFS.)

Dogs Head Dome, partially shaded at upper left, was formed about 2,100 years ago, while the Sugar Bowl Dome, shaded and lower to the right, was formed about 1,150 years ago. This photograph was taken below Timberline in 1964 or 1965. (USFS.)

In 1937, the Longview Ski Club members built this rustic cabin near Timberline, which could sleep several people. They also had a snowcat that was used to tow skiers from the end of the plowed road up to their lodge, which was later sold to Harry Truman. There were reportedly no teetotalers in the club, and relations with Truman were generally—but not always—pretty good. A shed built later housed the engine that operated the club's rope tow.

The snowcat that the club purchased in 1947 was able to tow 10 Nordic skiers near Timberline below Dogs Head, otherwise it was an eight-mile climb from Spirit Lake up to the club's cabin at Timberline. That uphill climb would be done with food and gear. (USFS.)

For a while, there was a proposal to establish a ski area on the north side of Mount St. Helens, but the avalanche threat proved too great, and members of the Longview Ski Club made do with their rope tow. This 1965 photograph looks down onto the turnaround at Timberline and north to Mount Rainier at left. (USFS.)

In this 1963 image, a late spring skier enjoys the view of Mount Adams from above Timberline on Mount St. Helens. (USFS.)

For Nordic skiers, the solitude and beauty of the snow-covered landscape is the attraction, as attested to by this 1963 photograph. (USFS.)

Winter remains a time to play in the snow at the mountain. Recreation takes many forms, including this moped pulling two people on sleds in a parking lot in 1961. (USFS.)

Snowmobiling has been and remains popular around Mount St. Helens. Prior to 1980, it allowed cabin owners access to their cabins when roads were buried under snow. (*The Columbian*; photograph by Steve Small.)

The Columbus Day storm of 1962 was a massive storm that first struck in northern California in the morning and then headed north along the coast, where it finally died out in southern British Columbia. The Mount St. Helens area was heavily impacted, and many trees were blown over. (USFS.)

This Boy Scout camp building was damaged by fallen trees from the Columbus Day storm. A massive clean-up effort was required before recreational facilities around Spirit Lake returned to being fully functional. (USFS.)

The Forest Service would seasonally relocate their offices from Spirit Lake to nearby Kelso during the winter. Because of the necessity of overseeing the cleanup from damage caused by the Columbus Day storm in the Spirit Lake basin, the Spirit Lake ranger's office was opened eight to ten weeks early, around April 1. During the Columbus Day storm at least 30 million board feet of lumber was blown down, according to a story in the March 31, 1963, issued of *The Oregonian*. There were 700 trees reportedly blown down along the highway within a mile of Spirit Lake. Above, youngsters are sitting on a log supervising the large machinery cleaning up storm damage. (Both, USFS.)

In late 2006, two large flood events caused widespread regional damage. At June Lake on the south side of the mountain, 15 inches of rain fell in early November and again in December during two seven-day periods. A lot of material was washed down, covering parking lots with debris and washing out roads. Major flood events frequently start with heavy, low elevation snowfalls being melted by warm, heavy rains that have their origins near Hawaii. The warm subtropical air is call the "Pineapple Express." (Both, Anderson.)

Snowfall at the 3,200-foot elevation of Spirit Lake is extremely variable. Two feet of snow covered the ground at Spirit Lake Campground on July 1, 1971, while in February 1973, snowmobiles were not able to use the Duck Bay road along the south shore because of a lack of snow. (USFS.)

This image shows a frozen Spirit Lake. (USFS.)

These men are shoveling snow from the front of the US Forest Service's ranger station at Spirit Lake after a particularly heavy snowfall. The roof has also been shoveled. (USFS.)

These men are digging out a van buried in deep snow at Spirit Lake. (USFS.)

Six

THE SOUTH SIDE

In 1905, Willis Vail climbed the ridge between Speelyai Creek and the Lewis River, near Yale, to capture this view. A lone homestead (at far right) stands in a clearing in the forest along what is now the Lewis River Road. Standing dead trees from the 1902 Yacolt Burn are visible; that fire was allowed to burn itself out. (Anderson, photograph by Willis Vail.)

Steam donkeys were used in logging operations throughout the Northwest; this one was in the Lewis River Valley. Cables, or hemp rope, would be attached to a log and pulled towards the donkey. When the donkey needed to be moved, the cable would be attached to a stump or rock, and the donkey would pull itself toward that location. (Walter Hanson; photograph by Wilfred Craik.)

A flume was constructed in the Lewis River valley to move railroad ties down to the town of Woodland. The ties were then sent from Woodland to The Dalles to be treated at the tie-treating plant, which is still located on the south side of the Columbia River. (Walter Hanson; photograph by Wilfred Craik.)

Lake Merrill was formed when a basalt lava flow came down the Kalama River canyon about 1,900 years ago and blocked a side canyon. These c. 1930 photographs show the ranger station that was established on the east side of the lake to facilitate management of state land in the area. The station was located on the present site of a recreation area on the east side of the lake. (Both, Washington State Digital Archives, photograph AR-28001001-Ph001386).

Monitor Ridge is in the center right of this c. 1907 view of the mountain. The Worm Flow complex is to the right. Many early postcards erroneously give the location of the mountain as Oregon rather than Washington. (Anderson.)

This view of Mount St. Helens, although not as iconic as that from the north side with Spirit Lake in the foreground, was also used for advertising purposes. In this case, it was used to promote an annual Rose Carnival in Portland, Oregon. (Steven Kinney.)

The photograph on this 1904 postcard was taken by James Waggener Jr. on the south side of the mountain in the mixed coniferous forest that covers the cave basalt; Waggener was probably near the entrance to Ole's Cave. (Anderson.)

Ole Peterson was well known to people living on the south side of Mount St. Helens. Peterson, a bachelor, lived at his ranch several miles east of the village of Cougar in the Lewis River Valley for 59 years. Around 1895, while out hunting, he found one of the entrances to a lava tube that is named after him—Ole's Cave. (Anderson.)

Wilfred Craik (at left with the case holding his glass plate negatives in the c. 1908 image above) had an amazing eye for photography. He tried to make a living at it, but unfortunately was not able to. The gentleman second from right, with the lantern, is possibly Ole Peterson, who may have been guiding this group to the cave he discovered. It was about a two-mile hike from Peterson's house to the cave entrance. Ole's Cave, or Peterson's Cave as it was sometimes called, was reportedly the first commercially developed cave in Washington. There are several lava tubes in the immediate area, but with the exception of Ape Cave, their locations are not publicized and entry is prohibited during the winter months to help protect hibernating bats. People are also asked to not enter the lava tubes if they have been in caves where white-nose syndrome is present, to help prevent the spread of that disease. (Both, Walter Hanson, photographs by Wilfred Craik.)

For quite some time, Ole's Cave was the most frequently visited lava tube in the Cave Basalt. It is over one mile long and was, thanks to Ole Peterson, Washington's first cave opened to tourists. Nearby Ape Cave was not discovered until about 1951. (Walter Hanson, photograph by Wilfred Craik.)

Lava tubes form in fluid basalt lava flows. While the surface may cool, much like ice on a river, the lava underneath remains hot and flows as long the eruption continues feeding lava to it. Skylights form either during the eruption or just after, when a section of roof collapses. The photograph for this postcard was possibly taken in 1903 by the Kiser brothers. (Anderson.)

US Forest Service officials stand at the entrance of Lake Cave in the Cave Basalt in this 1964 photograph. (USFS.)

The temperature in the caves now remains a steady 42 degrees Fahrenheit all year. At least one insect species was first described in the lava tubes here. Many of the caves in the area also provide vital winter hibernation sites for bats. (USFS.)

Ape Cave was discovered in 1951 when Lawrence Johnson, a logger working in the area, noticed a tree that did not look right. He investigated and saw that it had grown in a large sinkhole. A short time later, Leonard Reese became the first person to touch the floor of Ape Cave, the third-longest lava tube in North America and the only one open to the general public. (Anderson.)

In this 1960s photograph, a US Forest Service ranger is inspecting damage to the privy at the Lava Cast trailhead. The site showcases tree molds in the basalt lava, one of which is big enough to crawl through. (USFS.)

The Red Rock Pass andesite lava flow is pictured here in 1963. For some time, the preferred climbing route on the south side went up to Butte Camp, which is visible at center left. (USFS.)

Butte Camp Dome is visible at left in this c. 1959 photograph. (Sloan.)

This is a c. 1908 view from the flat on the north side of Butte Camp Dome, near Timberline. The elevation is about 4,200 feet. The forest looks like other forests found on nearby peaks at elevations closer to 6,000. (Walter Hanson; photograph by Wilfred Craik.)

Hikers planning on climbing the mountain from the south side would commonly head up the southwest side to Butte Camp, which was located next to Butte Camp Dome, one of the domes that was extruded early in the geological history of Mount St. Helens. Above the dome, it was then a fairly steep hike to the top through loose pumice and snowfields. (USFS.)

This photograph of the southwest side of the mountain above Butte Camp Dome was taken around 1963. (USFS.)

Although there were a few mudflows that came down the west side of the mountain in 1980, the eruption had relatively little impact on this side compared with what happened on the north face. This c. 2009 photograph shows the Butte Camp Dome from the slopes of the mountain. (Anderson.)

This early photograph shows the lava flows on the southwest side of the mountain above Butte Camp Dome. (USFS.)

Goat Mountain (elevation 4,965 feet), located on the west side of Mount St. Helens, is visible above the low clouds in this c. 1960 photograph taken during a climb from the north side. Goat Mountain is much older than Mount St. Helens, having been emplaced between 470,000 and 3 million years ago, while Mount St. Helens started forming within the last 40,000 years. (Sloan.)

Goat Mountain dome rises above the upper Kalama River drainage in this 1959 image. A forest composed mostly of lodgepole pine covers lahar deposits emplaced in the late 1400s. Some of the nearby relict stands of old growth forest contain some of the largest remaining noble fir. (Sloan.)

These two pictures of Goat Marsh show the contrast between how the same area appeared pre-eruption and in 2012. Goat Marsh is a federal Research Natural Area that protects the large marsh and a variety of forest types ranging from a depauperate lodgepole pine forest to a very productive noble fir forest. The marsh was formed about 300 or 400 years ago during the growth of the Summit Dome, when lahars blocked the outlet to Cold Spring Creek. That period of activity gave the mountain its pre-1980 form and height. (Above, Sloan; below, Anderson.)

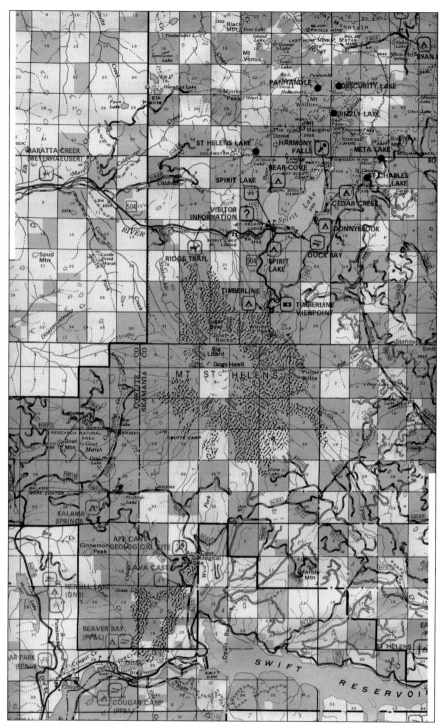

The Pacific Railroad Act of 1862 gave large amounts of public land to railroads to build transcontinental lines. Every other section of land would be given to the railroad, while the government would keep the rest. This created a checkerboard pattern of landownership, remnants of which still exist today. This image is from the 1973 Gifford Pinchot National Forest map.

In this 1981 image, the section lines that are also property lines clearly stand out. The Mitten lava flow is at upper right, while the base of Butte Camp Dome is at upper left. The surface of the Swift Creek lava flow is visible at right. Flow features on the Swift Creek flow, the largest lava flow in the history of Mount St. Helens, are visible at lower right. This flow formed about 17,000 years ago.

Prior to the eruption, logging on the south side of the mountain involved clearing most of the old-growth timber. This scene is just below the Worm Flows on the southeast side. Workers were replanting trees south of the mountain on the morning of May 18 when Mount St. Helens erupted; they survived the eruption because the blast went north.

Two hikers cross the Muddy River fan below the Shoestring Glacier sometime in the 1920s or 1930s. The upper Muddy River fan is subject to glacial outwash and winter storm flooding. The source of Shoestring Glacier was the Summit Ice Field, which was deposited in the Toutle River Valley and subsequently melted to form the large mudflow that traveled all the way down to the Columbia River. (USFS.)

This c. 1970 image looks up the Muddy River and Shoestring Glacier fans on the southeast side of the mountain. The land in the foreground is a mixed, fairly young open forest when compared with the much older, darker, mostly coniferous forest on the ridgeline to the right. (USFS.)

Shoestring Glacier, one of 11 named glaciers on the mountain, was fed by the summit icecap and extended downslope for about two miles from the summit. At the beginning of the 1980 eruption, a pyroclastic surge composed of superhot rock and gases melted almost 30 feet of glacial ice and snow from the surface of Shoestring Glacier, causing a large lahar. That lahar removed all trees in its path from the Muddy River fan and flowed down the Muddy River, exposing Lava Canyon, and down Pine Creek towards the Lewis River Valley. (USFS.)

The lahar that was formed at the beginning of the 1980 eruption had enough momentum to wash up and over a 124-foot-high ridgeline (visible in the foreground). Trees are beginning to recolonize the surface of the 1980 mudflow; however, winter flood events are preventing regrowth on some of the surface. This photograph was taken in 2004. (Anderson.)

526—NORTHWESTERN SCENES—CASCADE SERIES.
GOAT GORGE, EAST SIDE OF MT. ST. HELENS.

Ape Canyon (called Goat Gorge on this postcard) was formed when a lava flow blocked a drainage. The stream cut through the ridgeline, forming a narrow canyon. Post–1980 eruption rock falls have slightly widened the canyon. The trail to the canyon is one of the most popular with mountain bikers and hikers in the Mount St. Helens National Volcanic Monument. (Anderson.)

A good communication network is essential to managing a large area of land. A radio relay station on Pumice Butte, located on the east side of Mount St. Helens, was installed in the 1960s. East Dome, thought to have been formed about 1,200 years ago, is to the right of the two workers. (USFS.)

Prior to May 1980, the Plains of Abraham were kept nearly tree-free by frequent winter avalanches off the east side of Mount St. Helens, as illustrated by this 1962 photograph. The 1980 eruption blast and pyroclastic flows removed all trees from around the Plains of Abraham. (USFS.)

This 2007 photograph shows that vegetation was still sparse near the summit of the Plains of Abraham. Remains of trees killed in 1980 are still visible. Recolonization by plants 30 years later produces rich wildflower displays in midsummer. Pumice Butte (visible right of center) was heavily impacted by pyroclastic flows. (Anderson.)

On Saturday, May 17, 1980, at about 1:30 in the afternoon, this was the view from about six miles from the summit on the south side of the South Fork Toutle River. The mountain was dark, with its snow and ice covered by ash. The bulge on the north side, which was formed by magma pushing up inside the mountain, was reaching the critical failure point. The large notch on the upper left slope is the top of the bulge. Goat Rocks is the outcrop farther down. The following morning, all this would suddenly be changed. (Both, Anderson.)

At 8:32 Sunday morning, May 18, the bulge on the north side collapsed, creating the largest landslide in recorded history. It also uncorked the mountain's plumbing. Instead of rising vertically, as it was thought it would, the initial eruption spread out in a horizontal blast. In the upper reaches of the South Fork Toutle River, the north side of the canyon was heavily impacted by the blast while the south side received little effect. The first large mudflow down the South Fork Toutle River started immediately with the eruption. After setting a new flood stage record just below Silver Lake, the mudflow reached the Cowlitz River at 1:00pm. Mudflows on the North Fork Toutle River didn't form until later in the day and were much larger than those from the South Fork Toutle River. These photographs were taken September 5, 1982. (Both, Anderson.)

The northwest face of the mountain is pictured here, with Mount Hood (in Oregon) visible at upper right. Named glaciers that are visible are, from right to left, Talus, Toutle, Wishbone, Loowit, Leschi, and Forsyth. The Goat Rocks Dome (to the left of Wishbone) was formed during activity that occurred between 1831 and 1857. (USFS.)

On the back pages of local newspapers on March 21, 1980, articles announced that a minor earthquake had been recorded under Mount St. Helens. A week later, the mountain reawoke with steams blasts and cracks across the north side of the summit. (USFS)

Northerly face of Mount St. Helens, Gifford Pinchot National Forest,
during an eruption, afternoon of April 1, 1980.

The small steam blasts and cracking mountain, in hindsight, were symptoms that a body of magma—a cryptodome—was forming inside the north side of the mountain. The intrusion continued until the north slope finally collapsed in the landslide that unleashed the eruption of May 18. (USFS.)

This marked-up photograph shows various named features on the mountain prior to 1980 as seen from the Timberline parking area. Virtually every feature to the right of Dogs Head and Sugar Bowl Dome are now gone. (USFS.)

The 1980 eruption started with an earthquake that helped trigger the landslide. Portions of the landslide went as far as 14 miles down the Toutle River. The landslide uncorked the magma, and an unexpected lateral blast raced outwards at speeds up to 300 miles per hour. Within 15 minutes, 230 square miles of land were devastated by the blast. The eruption cloud reached an elevation of 15 miles within 15 minutes. (USFS.)

Spirit Lake was formed by sudden geologic events like that which happened in May 1980. The landslide that hit the lake in 1980 caused a tsunami that washed up the mountain's slopes behind the lake. The backwash brought with it the trees that had been growing on those slopes and deposited them in the lake basin, where they can be seen floating on Spirit Lake in this photograph from May 15, 1982. (Anderson.)

The forest in the upper Clearwater Creek drainage was blown over during the first 10 minutes of the 1980 eruption. In this June 1980 photograph, the east slope of Mount St. Helens, about 10 miles away, is visible in the upper right corner. (Anderson.)

Visible in this March 1982 aerial view are Mount Margaret in the left foreground and a feature called "The Dome" at center right. In the background, nine miles away, is the steaming crater of Mount St. Helens. A dome-building eruption in March 1982 added 4.4 million cubic yards to the dome in the crater. The two large linear bare spots below the crater were kept free of snow for several years because of the presence of hot rocks, which have since cooled. (Anderson.)

In August 1982, a dome-building eruption added six million cubic yards of lava to the dome. The circled helicopter gives scale to the growing lava dome. By the end of 1986, the dome had grown to 97 million cubic yards of lava. Activity quieted for 18 years, and in 2004, a mostly dome-building eruption began that lasted into January 2008 and added 121 cubic yards to the dome. (Anderson.)

As shown in this 1985 image, the landscape north of the mountain still looked pretty desolate five years after the eruption. However, the portion of the blast zone that was left untouched is a unique habitat found nowhere else. Thirty years after the eruption, most of the downed logs in this scene had decayed and returned their nutrients back to the soil. (Anderson.)

In this 1988 photograph, a steam blast cloud rises several miles above the mountain. This view from Norway Pass north of the mountain overlooks a log-covered Spirit Lake. (USFS; photograph by Roland Emetaz.)

Mount St. Helens is a mountain of fire and ice. It is impossible to predict what type of volcanic activity will take place next, or when. The mountain will reawake and will again surprise us. It will leave its mark on the landscape and on the people who live and play around it. Maybe in 200 years, large, old coniferous trees will again blanket the slopes around Spirit Lake. Hikers today can still visit Spirit Lake via the Harmony Trail, possibly imagining the ghostly laughter of children as it echoes from the water. Visitors and historians alike can remember and see what the mountain and the lake at its foot were like before 1980, thanks to the images made by so many photographers. (USFS.)

BIBLIOGRAPHY

Colasurdo, Christine. *Return to Spirit Lake*. Seattle, WA: Sasquatch Books, 1997.

Decker, Barbara. *Mount St. Helens: The Rebirth of Mount St. Helens*. Mariposa, CA: Sierra Press, 2007.

Foxworthy, Bruce L. and Mary Hill. "Volcanic Eruptions of 1980 at Mount St. Helens, The First 100 Days." Geological Survey Professional Paper 1249. Washington, DC: US Government Printing Office, 1982.

Guggenheim, Alan. *Spirit Lake People, Memories of Mount St. Helens*. Gresham, OR: Salem Press, 1986.

Harris, Stephen L. *Fire Mountains of the West: The Cascade and Mono Lake Volcanoes*. Missoula, MT: Mountain Press Publishing, 2005.

Jackson, Leland with Trudy Howarth. *An Early History of Spirit Lake & The Toutle River Valley*. Gig Harbor, WA: Red Apple Publishing, 1995.

Lembersky, Mark. *Mount St. Helens, Images of an Unexpected Landscape*. Portland, OR: Blue Heron Publishing, 2000.

Lipman, Peter W. and Donal R. Mullineaux. "The 1980 Eruptions of Mount St. Helens, Washington." Geological Survey Professional Paper 1250. Washington, DC: US Government Printing Office, 1981.

McClure, Rick and Cheryl Mack. *For the Greatest Good, Early History of Gifford Pinchot National Forest*. Seattle, WA: Northwest Interpretive Association, 2008.

NWIA Trail Guide, Mount St. Helens National Volcanic Monument, Gifford Pinchot National Forest. Northwest Interpretive Association, 2004.

Pringle, Patrick T. *Roadside Geology of Mount St. Helens National Volcanic Monument and Vicinity*. Olympia, WA: Washington Department of Natural Resources, 2002.

Williams, Chuck. *Mount St. Helens, A Changing Landscape*. Portland, OR: Graphic Arts Publishing, 1980.

There is a wealth of information on Mount St. Helens both online and in printed form. Several of these books are no longer in print but can still be found online through various sources.

For online information, search the Internet to locate websites for:
Mount St. Helens National Volcanic Monument, Gifford Pinchot National Forest
Mount St. Helens Institute
Cascades Volcano Observatory, U.S. Geological Survey
Pacific Northwest Seismic Network

Discover Thousands of Local History Books Featuring Millions of Vintage Images

Arcadia Publishing, the leading local history publisher in the United States, is committed to making history accessible and meaningful through publishing books that celebrate and preserve the heritage of America's people and places.

Find more books like this at
www.arcadiapublishing.com

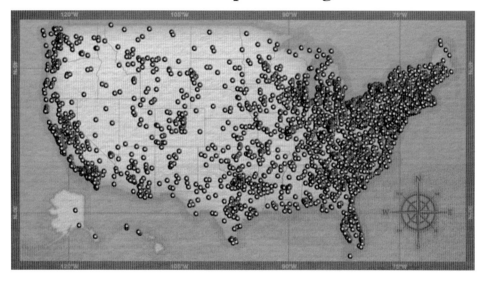

Search for your hometown history, your old stomping grounds, and even your favorite sports team.

Consistent with our mission to preserve history on a local level, this book was printed in South Carolina on American-made paper and manufactured entirely in the United States. Products carrying the accredited Forest Stewardship Council (FSC) label are printed on 100 percent FSC-certified paper.

MADE IN THE USA